MONTLIGHT PUBL

REIVERS

ANGLO-SCOTTISH BORDER RAIDERS
FROM THEIR ORIGINS TO THE END OF THE 16th CENTURY

KEITH DURHAM & ANGUS McBRIDE

Published in 1998 by Montlight Publications, a subsidiary company of Montvert Publications

Montlight Publications, PO Box 25, Stockport SK5 6RU

Montvert Publications, 2 Kingswood Grove, Reddish, Stockport SK5 6SP

Montvert (Distribution), PO Box 25, Stockport SK5 6RU

ISBN 1-874101-51-5

A CIP catalogue record for this book is available from the British Library.

Typeset by MONTSET Stockport Cheshire

Printed and bound under the auspices of MONTVERT PUBLICATIONS Stockport Cheshire

Dedication:-
For Andrew and Gayle

Editor: Dr Philip Greenough

CONTENTS

5. INTRODUCTION

7. THE FORGING OF THE BORDERLAND

12. THE BORDER MARCHES

14. BASTLES, TOWERS AND PELES

19. PRICKERS, BORDER HORSE AND FLODDEN FIELD

23. RAIDING

28. LIFE ALONG THE BORDER

32. REIVING NAMES

35. HOT TROD

37. WARDENS

38. DAYS OF TRUCE

42. THE BREAKING OUT OF KINMONT WILLIE

44. THE UNION OF THE CROWNS

46. THE LAST GOODNIGHT

48. FURTHER READING & MUSEUMS

REIVERS

"evell desposed people, great theeves inclined to wildness and disorder - a martiall kind of men who will be Scottishe when they will and English at their pleasure"

< opposite

A Moonlight Raid

Snow has fallen in the Border hills, and a band of well armed reivers thunders towards a lonely tower house, or *pele*. The defenders have fired a warning beacon on the battlements, alerting neighbours that raiders are approaching. Around the base of the tower is a *barmkin* wall, and, outside of this, a cluster of lowly dwellings from which ragged inhabitants dash towards the safety of the *barmkin* gate, defenders frantically beckoning them in.

INTRODUCTION

The Border reivers' origins were firmly rooted in the state of constant rivalry, bursts of open warfare, and political tensions which existed between the crowns of England and Scotland until the end of the 16th century. The Borderland became their battleground and each side encouraged its own Borderers to raid and harass their erstwhile neighbours across the line. This war of attrition created a region torn by a vicious cycle of raid, reprisal and blood feud, the Border Marches soon becoming a charred and dangerous wasteland. Survival became the name of the game and the Borderer evolved into a professional rustler and guerilla soldier, skilled in the art of raiding, tracking and ambush. He was a fine light horseman but was also prepared to murder remorselessly and run large scale protection rackets, giving the word *blackmail* to the English language.

THE FORGING OF THE BORDERLAND

"a martiall kind of men"

From the time Hadrian built his Wall as a barrier against the wild Caledonian tribes to the north, the 'Border' became a political and military reality. Following the disintegration of the Roman Empire the powerful Anglo Saxon kings of Northumbria extended their kingdom from the Humber to the Forth but by the 10th century their power had been broken by the Viking invasions, and the Scots, seizing the advantage, defeated the English at the Battle of Carham in 1018 and drove them back to the Tweed.

Following the defeat of the English at Hastings in 1066 the people of the north rebelled against Norman overlordship and it was William the Conqueror who brought the first taste of wholesale devastation to the Borderland. Marching northwards to quell the rebellious population, he left the Border region a charred wasteland, setting an ominous precedent for centuries to come. Initially the Scottish king, Malcolm Canmore, stood ready to oppose him but rather than face confrontation he erred on the side of caution and offered his submission for peace. His promises, however, were short lived, and whilst on one of his frequent raids into Northumberland, he was slain at Alnwick in 1093.

<opposite

Days of Peace

In the early days, sharing a common culture and landscape gave the Border folk of both kingdoms much in common with each other. With the exception of the occasional quarrel, they lived together in a rough kind of harmony

After a few decades of relative peace, David I of Scotland mounted an invasion into Northern England in 1138 but he was defeated near Northallerton at the Battle of the Standard. Surprisingly enough, the English king, Stephen, still conceded large areas of his northern kingdom to David, and the Scottish king was able to hold court in Carlisle and Newcastle. However, in the face of strong intimidation from Henry II in 1157 the Scots were forced to relinquish their hold on northern England.

A few years later, in 1173, when William of Scotland marched across the Border in an attempt to regain the lost territory, he was taken prisoner in a minor skirmish near Alnwick Castle. His ransom cost the Scots dearly, for the towns of Jedburgh, Roxburgh and Berwick were ceded to the English. As fate would have it they were soon in Scottish hands again when Richard the Lionheart sold them back to fund his crusades.

Throughout most of the 13th century the Borderland enjoyed a period of peace and prosperity. Border towns flourished, and landowners, hillfarmers and fishermen settled into a rhythm of life they had almost forgotten existed. But, as we shall see, all this was brought to an abrupt end during the reign of Edward I.

overleaf>

Edward I's Army on the Rampage

Soldiers of Edward I indiscriminately loot and pillage a Border village.

In 1286 Scotland's heirless King Alexander III was killed in a riding accident. The English had taken advantage of the peace, strengthening their Border fortresses of Norham, Wark, Alnwick and Carlisle, and had developed efficient lines of communication along their northern frontier. Edward I's policy was unequivocally expansionist, his aim being the complete annexation of Scotland, and so in the absence of an adult heir to the Scottish throne Edward used his influence to install John Balliol as his puppet ruler of Scotland. His attitude, however, became so overbearing that even the weak Balliol eventually rebelled and laid siege to Carlisle. In 1296, in an act of calculated retaliation considered brutal even in those times, Edward stormed Berwick putting 7,000 men, women and children to the sword, and begetting himself the name "Hammer of the Scots". By devastating the Scottish Borderland he hoped to terrify the Scots into submission, but what his ruthlessness actually achieved was a strengthening of Scots' resolve, which manifested itself in the shape of William Wallace. Soundly defeating the English army at Stirling Bridge in 1297, Wallace wreaked havoc on the northern shires but eventually Edward defeated him at Falkirk.

English plans for the domination of Scotland were soon to flounder. When the ineffective Edward II succeeded his father to the throne, a Scottish knight, Robert the Bruce, rose against him, and gathering the Scottish nobles to his cause annihilated Edward's army at Bannockburn in 1314. Berwick fell to Bruce in 1318 and his vengeful Scottish armies raided deep into Northern England, demanding blackmail and tribute from the local populace and exacting brutal retribution on those who stood against them. On Bruce's death, Edward III defeated the Scots at Halidon Hill, recapturing Berwick in 1333. Later, in 1388, the Scots secured a costly victory at Otterburn, and in 1402 the English took their revenge at Homildon Hill.

Sporadic raids and armed incursions by both nations continued, culminating in the greatest Border battle of them all, at Flodden Field, in 1513. To the Borderer, however, it was of little consequence which king was victorious, for the armies of both nations, whether retreating or invading, stole his cattle and crops, butchered his loved ones and left his homeland a scorched and impoverished wasteland. To make matters worse both governments, in an attempt to wear down the opposition, encouraged their Borderers to make raids on their embattled neighbours in the opposite realm, and as the years wore on, even in periods of comparative peace, an appalling cycle of raid, reprisal and outrage became the accepted way of life. The sight of ragged bands of riders thundering out of the darkness with fire and sword became a familiar and terrifying sight, and in response to the continued violence fortified buildings sprang up across the Borderland. The ability to survive in what was effectively a war zone became the very essence of the Borderer's precarious life.

opposite >

Scottish Retribution

Scots raiders attack the English Borders, settling old scores and terrorising the local population.

THE BORDER MARCHES

"... for the good of peace and better maintenance of ... good rule upon the Marches of both realms"

Realising that their constant warring across the Borderland had created a dangerously anarchic society, both governments, in an attempt to impose some degree of formality on the region, came to an agreement in 1249, known as the Laws of the Marches. By its conditions both governments split their frontiers into East, West and Middle Marches, and appointed Wardens to govern and police the unruly inhabitants. It was also acknowledged in the agreement that the standard laws of the land, proving woefully inadequate, were to be supplemented by a unique code of justice known as the Border Laws. These laws were specific to behaviour along the Borderline, and covered such offences as aiding and abetting raids into one's own country, illegal marriage to a person of the opposite realm, and the lawful recovery of stolen goods.

Since the end of the 12th century the Borderline, though often disputed, remained much as it is now. Beginning on the rocky Berwickshire coast in the east, it runs in a south-westerly diagonal, initially following the Tweed and then marching across the green, rolling Cheviot Hills. Following the Liddle Water and then the Esk it skirts Gretna and sinks in the bleak salt flats that fringe the Solway Firth.

The **Scottish East March**, bordered to the north by the Lammemuirs and to the south by the Tweed, included the broad fertile plain known as the Merse. Less aggressive than its neighbouring Marches it was much troubled by raids from both Scots and English reivers. The Warden's office was usually held by the Humes. Facing it was the **English East March**, stretching from Berwick upon Tweed to the Hanging Stone on Cheviot. The castles of Wark and Norham guarded crossing points on the Tweed whilst Bamburgh defended its coastline. A succession of Wardens ,including the Earl of Bedford and Henry, Baron Hundson, 'governed' from the garrison town of Berwick upon Tweed.

Comprising the Sheriffdoms of Roxburgh, Peebles and Selkirk, the **Scottish Middle March** faced the Cheviot Hills and extended west to Kershopefoot. It also included the valleys of Teviotdale and Liddesdale, home to notorious Border reiving families, such as the Armstrongs and Elliots who repeatedly launched raids into all three English Marches. In an effort to check the Liddesdale freebooters a Keeper, or additional Warden, was appointed, his residence being the grim and forbidding Hermitage castle. The Wardenry was generally held by the Kerrs of Ferniehurst and Cessford, who held their courts at Jedburgh and Hawick. Facing them across the Cheviots, and containing most of Northumberland, was the **English Middle March**. Here lay the unruly districts of Redesdale and Tynedale where the Robsons, Charltons and Dodds were habitual raiders both in their own country and Scotland. Defended by the castles of Harbottle, Warkworth and Alnwick, Wardens included Sir John Forster and members of the Percy family.

With Dumfries as its judicial centre, the defence of the **Scottish West March** lay in the hands of the powerful Maxwells who held the Wardenry for much of the 16th century. Comprising Eskdale, Annandale and Dumfriesshire its fortresses included Caerlaverock, Lochmaben and Langholm. The main centre of defence in the **English West March** was Carlisle where the Wardenry was held by the Dacres and, near the end of the 16th century, by the Scropes. Comprising Westmorland and Cumberland and running from Kershope to the Solway its castles included Naworth, Askerton and Bewcastle.

below

Map of the Marches

The Marches of England and Scotland, circa 1550.

Between the boundaries of both Western Marches lay a strip of territory ten miles long and three miles wide. Named the **Debateable Land** it had been argued over by both nations for centuries and was recognised as belonging to neither. As a consequence both governments refused to accept responsibility for the actions of the inhabitants and inevitably the Debateable Land attracted outlaws, fugitives and the powerful Grahams, who settled in and around it. With an arrogant disregard for authority they plundered each country with impunity. Eventually both governments agreed to set up a joint Commission which divided the Debateable Land by means of a rampart of earth known as the Scots Dyke. Although the issue was settled to the satisfaction of both nations the name lingered on, and the nefarious inhabitants, unimpressed, resumed their raiding with new vigour.

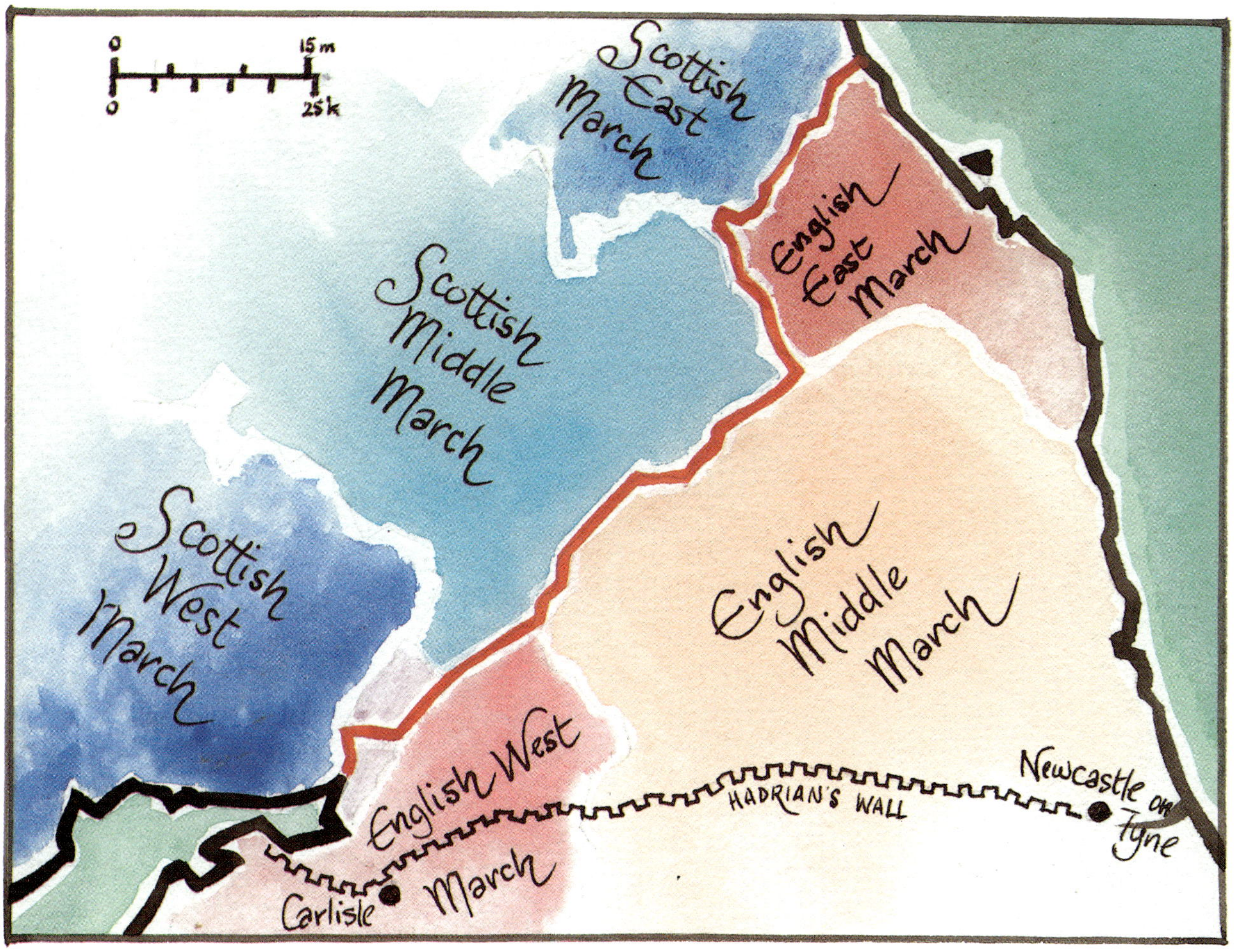

BASTLES, TOWERS AND PELES

"not a man amongst them of the better sort hath not his little tower or pele."

Whilst virtually anyone living within the six Border marches was prone to attack, families living within 20 or 30 miles of the Borderline were destined to bear the brunt of both incessant raiding and the brutal scavenging of invading armies. Not surprisingly then, dwellings within this narrow strip of land were constructed with the emphasis firmly on defence.

The commonest of these was the fortified farmhouse known as a *bastle*, a corruption of the French *bastille*, a fortified place. Generally built by the better-off farmer, the bastle was a stone-built two-storied, rectangular structure, measuring approximately 30-35 feet long by 20-25 feet wide. Standing about 20 feet high with walls between 3-4 feet thick, it was an immensely strong structure. Most bastles generally incorporated a barrel-vaulted basement, which supported the upper floor where the farmer and his family would live. A small sturdy door set at ground level in the gable-end wall gave external entry to the basement and, in times of trouble, it was here that the Borderer would lead his horses and cattle, bolting the door behind him. He then gained access to his living quarters via a small trapdoor set into the basement ceiling which could be bolted and locked from above. The main external door to the bastle was set high above ground level and was only accessible via a ladder, which the inhabitants would draw up after them. As a rule, bastles would have no more than two or three narrow barred windows, these being set high up in the walls. In the living quarters, floors were flagged with stone, and one wall usually accommodated a large open fireplace. It would seem that roofs were occasionally thatched but in most instances stone tiles fixed with sheep bones were utilised, thus minimising the risk of fire.

A more prestigious option available to the wealthier Border laird or headman was the fortified tower house. Originating from crude wood and turf strongholds which were surrounded by wooden palisades or "pales" (hence the term *peles*) the tower house was generally built in a highly defensible position and was usually enclosed by a substantial perimeter wall known as a *barmkin*. Inside this wall could be found various secondary dwellings which may have accommodated the headman's followers. The tower generally took the form of a rectangle averaging 30 feet by 45 feet, and was constructed with massive strong walls of stone between 5 and 10 feet thick.

Reaching heights of around 60 feet, towers invariably included a barrel-vaulted basement and two or more upper storeys. As a rule, the basement would be used for storage, but in an emergency it could be used to house horses and cattle. Entry into the tower was via a small doorway in the basement wall which was defended by two doors, the first of solid oak, the second a lattice work of iron bars, known as a *yett*.

opposite>

Bastle Attack

Reivers viciously attack the door of a bastle. Even such strong defences as these could not always withstand sheer brute force.

Well above ground level, small narrow windows and gun loops pierced the walls and a spiral or *newel* staircase gave access to the upper floors. Rising in a clockwise direction, these staircases were built into the thickness of the walls and were constructed in such a way that should the doors be breached and swordplay ensue, the advantage of manoeuvrability would always stay with a right-handed defender. The first floor provided living accommodation for the inhabitants and usually featured a substantial open fireplace and, occasionally, window seats. The Border lord and his family slept above, on the second floor where also would be found the *garderobes* or toilets. The top floor gave access to the roof and walkway, which was enclosed and protected by battlements. Roofs were sharply angled and covered with stone tiles, and the chimney usually sported a brazier, which would be fired on sight of raiders.

Though they were an obvious deterrent to small marauding bands of reivers, towers and bastles could still be overcome, either by way of a determined assault by a large force, by prolonged siege or by "*scumfishing*". This involved breaking down the outer doors and piling wet straw into the doorway and stairwell. This was then fired in an attempt to smoke the defenders into submission.

Many towers and bastles still survive, standing in mute testimony to their strength and durability, some of them still being inhabited to this day. Austere and forbidding in aspect, they stand as grim monuments to three turbulent centuries of Border warfare.

The following is a by no means complete list of some of the extant towers and bastles to be found on or near the Border. Those places preceded by a + symbol are open to the public:-

Towers

-Vicars Peel, Corbridge, Northumberland

-Elsdon, Redesdale, Northumberland

+Aikwood, Ettrick Bridge, Selkirk

+Smailholm, Kelso, Roxburghshire

+Drumcoltran, Dumfriesshire

+Orchardton, Dumfriesshire

-Greenknowe, Gordon, Berwickshire

-Hollows, Cononbie, Eskdale

-Fourmerkland, Dumfriesshire

Bastles

-Gatehouse, Bellingham, Northumberland

+Woodhouses, Holystone, Northumberland

-Hole, Bellingham, Northumberland

-Doddington, Wooler, Northumberland

+The Reivers Trail, Tarset, near Bellingham takes in a number of ruined bastles including:

Shilla Hill,
Black Middens,
Waterhead and
Barty's Pele.

opposite>

Bastles, Towers and Peles

Cross-sections showing the design and construction of two well fortified tower houses and a humbler bastle.

PRICKERS, BORDER HORSE AND FLODDEN FIELD

"a ruder more lawless crew there need not be, ... light cavalry, probably the very best in Europe"

Whilst usually engaged in trying to apprehend the reiver, both governments were actively aware of his military potential, and in times of national conflict eagerly recruited him into the ranks of their armies. Borderers would generally join an army as it passed through their territory, and, serving as light horsemen or *prickers*, would scout ahead of the main force, sack the enemy's villages, burn his crops, take prisoners and harass his lines of communication. Needless to say, plunder, ransom and self preservation were foremost amongst the Borderers' priorities, and in an attempt to impose some degree of loyalty and discipline, Border headmen were often allowed to retain command of their unruly retainers. As can be imagined, this very often turned out to be a double-edged sword - on occasion literally so!

<opposite

The Battle of Pinkie

Even in the midst of battle, such as at Pinkie in 1544, Borderers were observed talking and signalling to their opposite numbers, and were accused of engaging each other only in mock combat, to avoid doing each other serious harm. National colours were displayed by way of coloured scarves or small cloth crosses, blue for Scotland and red for England. These were tacked so loosely to their clothing that they could be dislodged by a "puff of wind" or at will by a non-committed Borderer!

The intermittent bursts of open warfare which ensued between England and Scotland were rarely allowed to interfere with the strong cross-Border alliances which existed between the reiving families. However, despite incidents like that at the Battle of Pinkie in 1544, where English and Scottish Borderers were accused of collusion, it would seem that when they were well led, Borderers acquitted themselves with distinction. This was particularly the case at the Battle of Solway Moss in 1542, when between 700-800 Cumberland *prickers* under the command of Thomas Wharton, Deputy Warden of the English West March, disordered and routed an invading Scottish army of over 10,000 men. English Border Horse campaigned with Henry VIII in France in 1544, where they were described as being probably the best light cavalry in Europe. They also served in Ireland in the 1570's, when the rebellions of O'Neill and Tyrone threatened English domination over that troubled isle. Skirmishing against an enemy as elusive and ruthless as themselves, many Borderers never lived to see their homeland again.

Perhaps the best and worst sides of the Borderers' character were displayed at the Battle of Flodden Field in September, 1513. In response to Henry VIII's invasion of France in July of that year, James IV of Scotland ,duty-bound by the Auld Alliance to support the French cause, launched a full-scale invasion across the River Tweed. With a well-equipped army of 40,000 men and some formidable artillery, he quickly took the castles of Wark, Norham, Etal and Ford, and set about devastating the surrounding countryside.

With Henry and the bulk of the English army in France, it was left up to Thomas Howard, Earl of Surrey and Lieutenant General of the North, to contain and repulse the Scottish invasion. Levying the northern shires as he marched towards the Border, Surrey arrived near Flodden with an army of 26,000 men. By the afternoon of the 9th September the Scots were drawn up in a strong defensive position on nearby Branxton ridge, and, due to a shrewd manoeuvre by Surrey, below them and blocking their line of retreat to Scotland, was the English army. Borderers served in both forces, the Scottish contingent being commanded by Lord Home, Warden of the Scottish East March, whilst the English fought under the Red Bull banner of the Dacres.

The Battle commenced with an exchange of artillery fire during which the Scottish ranks were badly raked by the English guns. In an attempt to escape this terrible pounding, the left flank of the Scottish army, including Home's Borderers, began to advance down Branxton Hill. Marching in huge phalanxes and armed with 18-foot pikes, they must have made a chilling sight. The English right flank was composed of contingents from Lancashire, Cheshire and Yorkshire, and, as the Scottish juggernaut rapidly approached, the majority of them broke and ran. The exultant Scots crashed into what was left of the defenders, but just as all seemed lost, Dacre's Border *prickers* rode into the fray stabbing and slashing at the exposed Scots' flank.

<opposite

The Battle of Flodden 1513

As night falls on the battlefield, English reivers cynically loot the baggage tents of their own countrymen.

As the initial Scottish attack ground to a halt and vicious hand-to-hand fighting intensified, James IV took the fateful decision to advance. Arming himself with a pike, and personally leading the main body of his army, which included the flower of Scotland's nobility, James marched down Branxton Hill. Advancing in close order and relying on the momentum of their pike formations to smash through the English ranks, the Scots had failed to notice a marshy ditch which ran along the bottom of the hill, and it was here that their attack came to grief. As the Scots became increasingly bogged down, the English infantry armed with lethal bill-hooks advanced. Chopping the points off the unwieldy pikes, they began to hack their way into the densely packed Scots. At the same time, Dacre and Home's bloodied forces, feeling their duty was done, drew apart, and, taking no further part in the battle, withdrew to their former positions, watching each other cautiously as the slaughter commenced. By nightfall, James, his nobles and 10,000 of his men lay dead or dying on the battlefield.

Scots and English reivers, behaving true to form, were soon looting the dead of both sides, the English even plundering their own army's baggage train and making off with goods, horses and cattle; according to the Bishop of Durham, they also spirited away many prisoners and ransomed them back to the Scots.

Both Home and Dacre were heavily criticised for their actions that day, and accused of collusion in order to minimise their casualties. They denied it, but, bearing in mind the Borderers' cynical attitude towards national allegiance, it was highly likely. The truth will probably never be known.

RAIDING

"famous for thieving, they are bred and live for theft ... spoyling others as they are spoyled"

As we have seen, by the beginning of the 16th century reiving had become a way of life. In order to survive in what had effectively become a battleground, many Borderers had become skilled and ruthless marauders. Born and raised in a war of attrition, they were hard men, devoid of pity and accustomed to a life of ambush, skirmish and pursuit. Cursed by all and sundry including the Church, they rode to keep their wives and "bairns" alive and, knowing no other way, willingly risked life and limb to do it. Coming from all levels of society, and often riding with the "wink" of approval from the very men appointed to stop them, they plundered across the six Marches and "shook loose the Border".

<opposite

Raiding

On occasion, some large-scale reprisal raids were undertaken with the March Wardens' unofficial blessing, and raiders, usually cloaked in anonymity, felt confident enough to carry their national colours into the opposite realm. Such an action could however cause a serious diplomatic rift between the two nations and provide an excuse for open warfare.

Raiding persisted throughout the year, but in late autumn, when days grew short and cattle were fat from summer feeding, frost hardened the land making it easier to drive stolen livestock across the wild and inhospitable terrain. This, then, was the reivers' "*chiefe time of stealing*". As the dark nights approached, peaceful Border folk rounded up their horses, cattle and sheep, and secured their dwellings. Warning beacons were prepared and armed watches were posted at river crossings and known "*theeves' roads*" or raiding routes. The local militia were put on full alert, and men slept with jack and lance close to hand. Even bridges and streets were chained against raiders but still they were not deterred .

Slipping over the Border on their sure-footed ponies, the reiving bands exploited their familiarity with the lay of the land and crossed the bleak moorland fells under cover of darkness. Picking their way through treacherous bogs and mosses, and fording rivers and swift-flowing burns, they navigated the twisting Cheviot passes by moonlight and came silently upon their victims in the dead of night. Striking swiftly, they rounded up any stray livestock and, if they had the force of arms to manage it, smashed their way into farmhouse or bastle. Murdering remorselessly and looting whatever pitiful goods or chattels they could lay their hands on, they burnt what they could not carry, and rode off with their stolen beasts and plunder, back into the darkness whence they came.

Raiding parties could number anything from perhaps half a dozen to sixty or a hundred, men, but there are many instances when, without warning, alliances of more than 2,000 lances thundered across the Border hills, their object being the large-scale plundering of a whole March. Sweeping down valleys and dales the raiders scattered what little resistance they encountered, sacking towns, hamlets and churches along the way. Contemptuous of the largely ineffective forces of law and order, these huge robber bands often terrorised the surrounding area for days, rustling thousands of sheep, cattle and horses, and amassing vast quantities of loot along the way.

As they began to drive the stolen livestock and plunder homewards, smaller raiding parties would be detached from the main host and despatched to "*spoyl*" and pillage any outlying hillfarms, burning any remaining crops as they went. Usually a rearguard was left behind to cover the retreat and to warn the main body of any serious pursuit.

It should be borne in mind that many raiding parties were made up of both Scots and English reivers, for, even though it could carry the death penalty, cross-Border marriage flourished and many Borderers. had like-minded kinsmen in the opposite realm.

<overleaf

A Great Raid

A huge reiving band on the loose. The Headman sits astride his *hobbler*, a recently slain deer slung across his saddle, whilst his companions drive cattle and sheep before them. Such scenes of depradation had become commonplace on both sides of the Border by the late 16th century.

Whilst most of the persistent raiding occurred close to the Borderline, Scottish reivers did on occasion extend their activities as far south as Newcastle and Penrith, and even the outskirts of Edinburgh were not safe from their English counterparts.

Some wardens were diligent enough to mount a pursuit, and many reivers ended their days on the gallows in Hexham, Carlisle, Newcastle or Jedburgh. On occasion, honest folk too put up a stout resistance and sometimes, no doubt, raiders ran into other reivers, characters as grim and determined as themselves, who would trade blow for blow and give no quarter. Such savage skirmishes would take their toll and many a reiving band must have returned home empty handed, with dead kinsmen slung across their saddles.

Not surprisingly, as time wore on, easy pickings across the Border became a thing of the past, and reivers began to make raids on their own countrymen. The Borderland became locked in a cycle of violence, and raids and reprisals followed one after another with destructive regularity, leaving in their wake bitter feuds which would haunt Border families for generations to come.

opposite>

Armour and Weapons

"Steill Bonnett, Jak and Hobbler"

Boldness, cunning and speed were the reiver's strengths, and his capacity to hit without warning and vanish without trace was largely due to his choice of weapons, armour and steed.

The 8-foot lance or *stave* appears to have been the commonest weapon available, and the reiver wielded it with deadly precision.

The ability to move swiftly was crucial to the reiver's activities, so he avoided weighing himself down with heavy armour. By the end of the 16th century he was wearing a light, open helmet known as a *burgonet*. Peaked and usually fitted with articulated cheek-pieces, these fine *steill bonnetts* came in both plain and decorated forms. Perhaps the most common helmets of the 16th century were the *Spanish morions* or *pikemen's pots* and the *combed morion* with its distinctive high comb and sharply curved brim.

Some Borderers, mainly the wealthy sort, carried a single-shot wheel-lock pistol known as a *dagg*. These were heavy, unwieldy pieces and though murderous at close range were generally inaccurate and slow to reload; and so, owing to the inadequacies of such primitive firearms, even near the end of the 16th century, it is not surprising that the trusted longbow was often still preferred.

There is evidence that some carried a studded shield or *targe*.

To protect the torso, some Borderers wore a steel cuirass or *back and breast* but most of them, rich and poor, put their trust in the *jack* or *jak of plaite*. Resembling a long, sleeveless waistcoat these garments were made up of layers of padded material between which were sewn small plates of iron, steel or horn. Often faced with leather or canvass, and comfortable to wear, particularly for horsemen, the *jack* was an effective protection against all but the most deadly blows.

From all accounts almost everyone carried a dagger. These ranged from crude but lethal home-made fighting knives to sophisticated parrying daggers designed to be used in conjunction with a sword.

He rode a small, sturdy horse, usually no more than 13-14 hands, known variously as a *hobbler*, *nagg* or *galloway*. Bred for endurance, these hardy little ponies, whilst carrying a fully armed man, could pick their way for mile after mile across the rugged Border terrain, and required little or no grooming.

Some fine broadswords have survived from the period, usually with blades approximately 3 feet long. Primarily for slashing, they were generally fitted with basket hilts which gave good protection to the hand.

Long leather riding boots protected his legs.

LIFE ALONG THE BORDER

"we are not acquainted with many learned or rare frazes"

Each time the reiver and his accomplices left their tower or bastle to run a foray, life for those left at home must have been full of uncertainty. Whilst anxiously awaiting the return of a husband, son or father, the women and children needed to be constantly alert to the threat of theft, raid or reprisal. In addition to living under this constant strain most Border folk lived frugal lives, scraping a precarious living by raising sheep and cattle and growing what food they could.

The very poor lived in squalid mud and wood hovels, whilst the better off as we have seen, dwelt in farmhouses, bastles or towers. Doubtless the womenfolk did their best to make these buildings a home for their families, but even in a well built tower conditions must have been Spartan to say the least. Bare stone walls may have been decorated with tapestries, and, curiously enough, carpets. Dried grass, herbs and heather covered the floor and furniture was generally confined to a sturdy bed, tables, benches and stools. The small windows in these fortified dwellings allowed little light to penetrate and families relied on torches and a single, large open fire to relieve the gloom.

Borderers lived on a fairly basic diet of wheat, barley and oats, from which biscuits could be made, supplemented with fish and cheese. Beef and mutton were boiled or roasted and, depending on how affluent the Borderer was, could be washed down with milk, ale or even wine.

According to contemporary accounts, Border folk were generally kind to travellers with whom they had no axe to grind, and their hospitality, though basic to southern eyes, was genuine enough.

Men and women alike dressed as best they could afford, though most clothing must have been somewhat rustic and hard-wearing. Some finery was in evidence however, usually in the shape of bonnets, cloaks and padded and slashed tunics, all of which must have added a welcome splash of colour.

Women were reported as being fair and comely and were generally well treated. There are numerous references to strong-minded "lasses" making their presence felt, such as the Charlton matriarchs, who served "the dish of spurs" to the "*heidman*" indicating that the larder was empty and it was time to be riding! Children, even those born out of wedlock, were cared for and raised in the strong traditions of their clan. Childhood, however, was brief and it was not unusual to find a twelve-year old riding out on a foray.

Professional medical help was scarce and difficult to find, and many folk who lived in the remoter areas had to rely on midwives and the physicians who travelled the Borderland applying poultices, extracting troublesome teeth and dressing wounds.

opposite >

Spur On The Dish

The lady of the house presents the headman, with the famous dish - much to his annoyance and to the amusement of the kitchen minions and hangers on. He will now have to go reiving!

In spite of his harsh and perilous lifestyle the Borderer did find time for recreation. He could wile away the long winter nights by playing at cards and dice or by listening to the small-pipes which would often accompany the reciting of stories and ballads, celebrating the high drama of raid, revenge, triumph and tragic death. Hawking and fishing helped fill the larder, and horse racing and football proved popular too, attracting participants from all social levels. It would seem that raids and acts of skulduggery were often plotted under cover of these sporting events, and ale houses, however crude, were usually full of thieves and as popular as ever.

Religion does not seem to have been a significant influence on the Borderers' lives, though it was reported that they prayed devoutly enough for good fortune before setting out on a raid. Superstition was rife and it was rumoured that on the Scottish border a child's fighting hand was left unchristened, thus allowing him to strike wicked and unholy blows on his enemies. Families did attend church but were not averse to bringing their weapons and quarrels with them, and services would sometimes end in a violent fracas. Small wonder the clergy went armed with sword and dagger.

Perhaps the most destructive custom on the Border was that of "deadly feud". Proud, belligerent and quick to take offence, the Borderer was fiercely loyal to his family and clan, for this was where his security lay. Due to the erratic or non-existent forms of justice available to him, the Borderer and his clan had become accustomed to seeking redress in their own way. Any attack or insult, however slight, to himself or any one of his kinsmen could bring swift and violent retribution. Scotts against Kerrs, Armstrongs against Robsons, Johnstones against Maxwells, Selbys against Grays, these feuds were enshrined in a warped code of honour, and vengeful fathers passed on their enmity to their sons. Habitual raiding and shifting alliances between families on both sides of the line ensured that there was always some incident to take offence at, and "deadly feud" thrived across the Border Marches. It was also no secret that some Border officers and even March Wardens were extremely reluctant to apprehend such offenders for fear of becoming involved in these deadly affairs.

In addition to all this, powerful riding families such as the Armstrongs and the Grahams ran sophisticated and highly lucrative extortion rackets, taking money, goods or crops in exchange for protection. Dealing savagely with any unfortunates who could not, or would not, meet their demands they terrorised the poor and weak and gave the word "blackmail" to the English language. No doubt some form of protection was given to the farmer who had been "*spoyled*" but it would normally take the form of helping mount a posse in pursuit of his stolen goods or livestock. Recognised under the Border Laws, this practice was known as the "Hot Trod".

opposite>

Blackmail

A party of reivers threaten a farmer outside his bastle and demand blackmail. The farmer's wife and children peer anxiously around the bastle door.

REIVING NAMES

"they run together in clans as they call it or names"

For reasons of security and strength in numbers, Borderers belonging to the great riding clans tended to settle in particular valleys and dales, for example the Armstrongs in Liddesdale, the Robsons in Tynedale, the Burns in Teviotdale, and so on.

Inevitably, with so many people of the same surname living in such close proximity, some confusion over individual identity was bound to arise, the problem being further exacerbated by successive generations overusing the same traditional Christian names. In an attempt to differentiate one man from another some Borderers were referred to via their parents names, hence Jock's Sandy, Christie's Will, The Laird's Jock; others were identified by their place of abode, such as Jock Of The Park, Wat O' Harden, Christie Of Barngleish.

The Borderer also delighted in bestowing witty, caustic and highly descriptive nicknames on his friends, foes and family. Some of these alluded to a character's physical appearance, such as Fingerless Will, Halflugs and Nebless (meaning noseless) Clem, whilst others could commemorate a narrow escape, as in Ill (half) Drooned Geordie, or the failed career of David Na Gud (meaning no good) Priest. We can only ponder the meaning behind As It Looks and All Our Eynds, but are left in no doubt as to the violent nature of Archie Fire The Braes, Thom With The Lance and Out With The Sword. There were of course many other equally colourful examples; these included Hob The King, Crack Spear, David The Lady, Dog Pyntle, Unhappy Anthon, Sore John, Wynking Will, Buggerback, Redneb, Bangtail, Pikehood, Andrew The Wooer, Halting Will, Jock Pott The Bastard, The Sweet Man, Crooked Pledge, Curst Eckie, and Jock With The Lippe.

A list of some of the most frequently found or particularly interesting Borderers' surnames is given on the opposite page. It should be noted that there are many alternative spellings not given here (for example Taylor for Tailor and so forth) and it would be a daunting task to list every variant.

Archbold
Armstrong
Beattie
Bell
Burns
Carleton
Carlisle
Carnaby
Carrs
Carruthers
Chamberlain
Charlton
Collingwood
Crisp
Croser
Crozier
Cuthbert
Dacre
Davison
Dixon
Dodd
Douglas
Dunne
Elliot
Fenwick
Forster
Graham
Gray
Hall
Hedley
Henderson
Heron
Hetherington
Hume
Irvine
Irving
Johnstone
Kerr
Laidlaw
Little
Lowther
Maxwell
Milburn
Musgrove
Nixon
Noble
Ogle
Oliver
Potts
Pringle
Radcliffe
Reade
Ridley
Robson
Routledge
Rutherford
Salkeld
Scott
Selby
Shaftoe
Storey
Simpson
Tailor
Tait
Trotter
Turnbull
Wake
Watson
Wilson
Woodrington
Yarrow
Young

HOT TROD

"to follow their lawful Trod with hound and horn and hue and cry"

At the height of the reiving season ,from October to the end of February, watches were reinforced and men slept uneasily. If marauders were sighted fray bells rang and a network of beacons were fired. These were strategically sited on hilltops and towers, and gave warning to adjoining districts that reivers were approaching. Communities were on full alert and men were quickly armed and in the saddle. If there were enough of them, they might deter or even repulse the reivers, but many raids were stealthy affairs and the alarm was only raised after the event.

If he was lucky enough to be still alive, the Borderer had the right within six days of being "*spoylt*", to mount a legal pursuit in order to reclaim his stolen goods. He was also entitled to enlist the support of his neighbours, who were duty bound to assist and ride with him in what was known under the Border Laws as the "Hot Trod". Few men desisted, for failure to "follow the fray" was punishable by heavy fine, or even death.

<opposite

The Hot Trod

The Warden's troopers, in pursuit of reivers, spot them in the valley below. The hounds are unleashed and a trooper sounds the horn. Another carries, aloft on his lance, a blazing turf - the sign that this is the *Hot Trod* and is legalised retribution.

Tracking dogs or "*slewe*" hounds were unleashed, and, as the posse thundered past homestead and tower, Border folk were able to recognise the riders as a legal Trod by the sounding of a horn, and by the blazing turf that one of the riders carried on the point of his lance. Most importantly, perhaps, the Trod was allowed to cross the Borderline fully armed in pursuit of the thieves, their only obligation being to inform the first person they encountered of the nature of their quest.

A dramatic sight they must have made, but retreating raiders, though handicapped by their stolen beasts and plunder, did not give in easily and often turned on their pursuers. Many a Trod must have ended this way, in a bloody moonlight skirmish, where broadsword and lance determined the final ownership of cattle and loot.

WARDENS

"men of estimation and nobility"

In the early days a Warden's duties were mainly concerned with the military defence of his March, but in time he became increasingly responsible for other functions, including the setting and maintaining of watches, ensuring that men assisted in the Hot Trod, holding Truce Days with his opposite number across the Border and ensuring that the fortifications within his March did not fall into decay.

Whilst civil offences were still dealt with by local courts, any infringement of the Border laws came under his jurisdiction. In these matters he held the power of life and death and any malefactor caught red handed could expect summary execution by beheading or hanging. He was also expected to staunch the flow of raiding and mount his own reprisals, but judging from the volumes of correspondence his duties generated, he must have spent at least as many hours bogged down in paperwork as he did chasing raiders across the Border hills. Most Wardens complained that the remuneration for what was an extremely difficult job was grossly inadequate, and, in addition, constantly pleaded with rather miserly government officials to forward the necessary funds needed for the repair of fortifications and payment of troops.

<opposite

The Warden

Dealing with voluminous correspondence was one of the Warden's more wearisome tasks. Here he sits at his desk, assisted by his clerk.

The Warden was, however, allowed sundry expenses, and lived in an official residence rent free. Assistance with his duties came in the form of a Deputy Warden, Land Sergeants, Keepers and Bailiffs, and he had, of course, a large body of troopers at his disposal. Apart from the obvious power and prestige of his position, the Warden could find lucrative ways to amass his own personal fortune. One of the most effective was the "*Warden Roade*". Launching a large scale incursion across the Border, ostensibly in order to teach persistent raiders a lesson, his troops would devastate their valleys, towers and crops, taking plunder, livestock and prisoners for ransom as they went. The Warden was legally entitled to half the value of whatever was brought back, the other half presumably being credited to the Crown. In addition, he was also entitled to a percentage of any fine he might impose for a minor offence. It was a fact of life, however, that some Wardens on both sides of the line became deeply involved with the families whose reiving they were supposed to curb, and simply used the office as a means to further their own ends.

Owing to the constant state of tension between the two crowns and the ever present threat of invasion, rumour and intrigue were rife. Spies and Government agents frequently crossed the Border Marches, and as a consequence Wardens were expected to sift through any information that happened their way, and pass anything of relevance on to central government. That the Warden's office carried with it a large degree of personal danger goes without saying and the lurking threat of invoking deadly feud in the course of his duties was always a possibility, particularly so at a Day of Truce.

DAYS OF TRUCE

"doe justice upon all complaints presented unto him"

If redress via the Hot Trod was unsuccessful and the thieves escaped with their loot, every Borderer who had been raided and "*spoyled*" had the opportunity to lodge his grievance and claim for compensation with the Warden's clerk. These claims or bills were to be heard and adjudicated upon at a Day of Truce. These were originally scheduled to take place once every month, or, at least, at regular intervals, but by the 16th century they were generally held as and when a Warden and his counterpart could agree upon a mutually acceptable date. Meetings were often "shot" or cancelled by one Warden or the other for a multitude of reasons, and sometimes as much as a year could pass before they discussed what, by then, had become a huge agenda.

Truce Days generally lasted from sunrise of the agreed day to sunrise of the next, and, during that time, safe conduct was assured for all those in attendance, except of course those unfortunates who were found guilty of their alleged offences. Occasionally, because of the sheer volume of business to be dealt with, the actual length of the Day of Truce had to be extended by mutual agreement to two or maybe three days.

It was the custom to hold these meetings on or near the Borderline at such places as Kershopefoot, Windy Gyle, Lochmaben, the Reidswire and Wark.

As we have seen, any criminal caught by the Warden in his own area of jurisdiction was swiftly dealt with or imprisoned but, in spite of his powers of pursuit, it was a risky business to try and arrest villains and their accomplices who had slipped across the Border and were well ensconced in their own towers or bastles. Wardens therefore presented their bills of complaint to their opposite number and it was his duty to apprehend the accused party and present him for trial at the Day of Truce. This was not always an easy task, as the accused could often be a man of high standing or of vicious temperament, and, because of the lack of secure gaols, Wardens often simply informed the accused party of their obligation to attend the Truce Day for trial and reminded them of the penalties for non-attendance. Needless to say, many nimble reivers who were due to appear simply ignored their "bail" and vanished into the neighbouring March or sought sanctuary with kinsmen in the opposite realm.

Wardens generally treated each other with due respect and once they and their retinues had arrived at the place of Truce formalities were observed and the proceedings could begin. Men could be tried either by the Wardens themselves or by a jury of twelve men, six Scots chosen by the English and six Englishmen of the Scots' choice. If the case against the accused was found not to be proved he was free to go and the bill against him was said to be "cleared". If, on the other hand, the Wardens or the jury found him guilty the bill was filed and marked "foul". Punishment would then be prescribed or, in its place, compensation would have to be paid to the injured party. If the accused was unable to pay this then he, or one of his relatives, might be taken into the opposite realm as a "pledge" until his family were able to find the required money or goods. If the matter was not resolved in a year then he could forfeit his life.

Finally, unfortunates who had been found guilty of a capital offence or March treason were duly sentenced to death and led off to execution. A proclamation was then read out detailing the findings of the court and everyone returned to their respective March.

Needless to say, Truce Days were an enormous source of entertainment for those not directly linked to the proceedings, and good Border folk and ruffians alike flocked to these occasions in their hundreds. Usually armed and wearing their best finery they took full advantage of the temporary safe conduct and, laying aside their differences, fraternised with both friends and enemies from the opposite realm, with whom they had so much in common. Horseflesh would be admired and many a bargain struck. Ale was available and acrobats, pedlars, gypsies and tinkers plied their trade. Men caught up with what was going on in the World, and argued over the merits of the longbow against those of the new-fangled handgun. Most Truce Days ended peacefully enough as was the intention, but unfortunately, as one might expect, they did on occasion get out of hand, sometimes by accident and sometimes by design, and the whole affair could end in mayhem and bloodshed.

One of the most famous of the Border Ballads had its origin in an incident, which is discussed in the next section, involving the violation of a Truce Day by the agents of Lord Scrope, the Warden of the English West March.

overleaf>

The Breaking Out of Kinmont Willie

Following the capture of Kinmont Willie in flagrant violation of the terms of Truce Days, a bold rescue operation was undertaken. Here the rescuing reivers, their mission accomplished, head for the River Eden - for their waiting horses and the safety of the Scottish Border.

THE BREAKING OUT OF KINMONT WILLIE

"I would fetch oute of England Kynmont, dead or alive"

Commemorated in one of the most popular of the Border Ballads, few episodes in Border history are as worthy of celebration as the Bold Buccleuch's rescue of Kinmont Willie from the Corbies' Nest (Carlisle Castle).

Hailing from the Scottish West March, Will Armstrong of Kinmont was the quintessential reiver, a notorious freebooter, who, in the best reiving traditions, had a foot firmly entrenched in each realm. Married to an English Graham, he was deeply in league with the Maxwells, who, despite being Wardens of the March encouraged his depredations across the Borderline. Riding out from their strongholds in the Debateable Land, Kinmont's "Bairns" as his marauders were known, rampaged extensively across the English West and Middle Marches, and, when the fancy took them, plundered indiscriminately in Scotland too. Often mentioned in connection with outrages and bills of complaint, Kinmont apparently led a charmed life. Protected by the powerful Maxwells, it was even rumoured that by causing so much havoc in England he was secretly favoured by the Scottish king, James VI. Ironically enough, in the events which were to ensure him his place in Border history, he was actually an innocent party.

Kinmont's arch enemy was Thomas, Lord Scrope, Warden of the English West March, where much of Kinmont's persistent raiding was carried out. The old ruffian and his accomplices had long flaunted Scrope's authority and were a permanent thorn in the harassed Warden's side. Frustrated by his failure to bring such a rank reiver to justice, Scrope's opportunity came unexpectedly when Kinmont Willie attended a Day of Truce held near Kershopefoot in March 1596. The day passed without incident, and Kinmont, who was probably there just as an observer, departed with a few friends in the company of the Scottish Deputy Warden. Though not present, Scrope was represented by his Deputy, Salkeld, and it was he who, with a force of troopers and in blatant violation of the terms of Truce, pursued and captured the redoubtable old reiver. Tied to his horse, he was led to Carlisle Castle and brought before Lord Scrope. Like most professional criminals Kinmont knew his rights, but in spite of his protestations he was imprisoned forthwith.

Word of what had happened spread quickly and Borderers of both nationalities were outraged at this flagrant breach of the Border Laws, none more so than Walter Scott of Buccleuch in whose area of jurisdiction the arrest had taken place. Keeper of Liddesdale and a formidable freebooter himself, the Bold Buccleuch was a fine exponent of feud and foray, and delighted in his reputation. Brave, resourceful, cruel and proud, Buccleuch took Kinmont's arrest as a personal insult to his office, and he dispatched a series of angry letters to Scrope, demanding Kinmont's immediate release. But Scrope had waited a long time to get his hands on Kinmont Willie Armstrong and no doubt hoped to see him mount the Carlisle gallows on Harraby Hill. Not surprisingly he dismissed Buccleuch's demands out of hand.

Realising Scrope would not give up his prisoner, Buccleuch decided to take the law into his own hands and mount a rescue attempt. Breaking into Carlisle Castle, probably the most secure fortress in the Border Marches would be an extremely dangerous undertaking and in order to carry it off he needed to recruit the very best Border riders he could find. All of those approached were well aware of the risks to life and limb and knew that their only reward would be the satisfaction of snatching their comrade from under Scrope's very nose. Buccleuch was not short of volunteers. Details of the rescue were finalised at Langholm Races and the raiders assembled at Morton, one of Kinmont's towers in the Debateable Land, as dusk fell on 13th April 1596.

And so, on that dark and stormy night, as Buccleuch gave the order to advance and rode off into the darkness, rain and legend, alongside him rode between 80 and 100 of the most wicked, brave and splendidly formidable rogues in Border history. Armstrongs, Elliots, Scotts and Grahams, they numbered in their ranks such veterans as Auld Wat of Harden, Christie of Barngleish, Willie Kange, the Chingles, the Young Laird of Whithaugh, John of the Hollows and Kinmont's own three sons - Geordie, Francie and Jock, expert reivers all. Eager to assist such an enterprise, the Grahams had also ensured a safe passage through their territory in the Debateable Land, giving the raiders a clear run at their target. Buccleuch's scouts reconnoitred ahead and were followed by an assault group carrying the ladders, crowbars and irons necessary to break into the fortress. Following behind them with the main body, Buccleuch and his raiders stealthily covered the ten miles to Carlisle, and, crossing the dangerously flooded river Eden, they arrived at the Corbies' Nest two hours before dawn. The terrible weather had forced the city Watch under cover and so, leaving a rearguard to cover their retreat, the raiders reached the walls undetected. Here they discovered their scaling ladders were too short, but, spotting a small postern gate still to be seen in the west wall, they quickly undermined it and were inside the walls, dealing swiftly with two startled guards. Buccleuch's informants in the castle had informed him exactly where Kinmont Willie was being held and whilst his raiders took up defensive positions around the postern gate a handful of them freed the old reiver. By now alarms were being sounded, Scrope was alerted and guards dashed to the west wall. But it was all to no avail; covered by their rearguard Buccleuch's raiders, with Kinmont in their midst, fell back to the Eden, re-crossed it and thundered back across the Border to the safety of their own realm.

Pursuit was pointless, and a devastated Scrope was left to account for the loss of his prize prisoner. Desperate to minimise his embarrassment he hugely exaggerated the size of Buccleuch's force and placed the blame squarely on his garrison's incompetence. The rescue caused a political furore between the two realms, and Queen Elizabeth demanded that Buccleuch be brought to justice. James VI managed to evade the issue for over two years but eventually Buccleuch was dispatched to the English Queen's court to explain himself. That Elizabeth was satisfied with his explanation is apparent by her comment that with 10,000 such men James could shake the firmest throne in Europe!

THE UNION OF THE CROWNS

"all rebels and disorderly persons will be prosecuted with fyre and sword"

Though they did not realise it, the men who rode out with Buccleuch to rescue Kinmont Willie on that stormy night in 1596 were destined to become the last of their kind, for their turbulent way of life was soon to come to an end.

As the 16th century drew to a close, reiving became so incessant that, in an attempt to check cross-border raiding, consideration was actually given to the idea of re-fortifying Hadrian's wall! It was, however, not to be necessary. On 24th March 1603, Queen Elizabeth I died and with her passing a new era was to dawn on the Borderland. The Grahams, Armstrongs and Elliots celebrated the news of her death with a massive raid into Cumberland, devastating as far south as Penrith, and "lifting" over 4,000 cattle. It was to prove their ultimate undoing, for, as James VI of Scotland travelled to London to inherit Elizabeth's crown and become James I, king of both realms, he issued a proclamation that would mark the beginning of the end. Furious at the recent outburst of anarchy in the Borders he threatened all those concerned, including their wives and "bairns", that they would be dealt with by "*fyre and sword*" and added a warning that the culprits would do well to throw themselves upon his mercy or face dire consequences.

Well aware of the lamentable state the Borders were in, James then introduced a number of far-reaching policies to eradicate the reivers and their turbulent way of life once and for all. There was now to be only one realm and the Marches would cease to exist. Even the word "Borders" was to be replaced with "Middle Shires".

Hence, in a single stroke, the ultimate sanctuary of being able to cross the Borderline and evade pursuit was denied to the reiver. Suddenly there was nowhere left to hide. The office of Warden was to be abolished and all towers and fortifications deemed unnecessary for the maintenance of law and order were to be dismantled. James also set up a commission consisting of six English and six Scottish officials. With his authorisation, and using what amounted to unlimited powers, they zealously began the pacification of the Borders.

The Border Laws, which both governments - and the reivers - had frequently used to their own ends, were abolished and the law of the land was to be obeyed by one and all. Courts were set up in the principal Border towns, and known reivers were quickly arrested. Execution without trial, known as "Jeddart (Jedburgh) Justice" was the order of the day and mass hangings soon became a common occurrence.

opposite >

The Union Of The Crowns

Mosstroopers watch uneasily from a hillside as their companions are subjected to "Jeddart Justice", following the reforms of James I.

THE LAST GOODNIGHT

"Mosse-troopers, thiefs and others wicked and lawless men"

Desperate to escape the King's wrath, Border lairds and headmen, including Buccleuch, joined in the purge of their former accomplices without a trace of conscience. The Grahams, Elliots and Armstrongs were singled out for particularly draconian treatment, many being executed out of hand, and others being forcibly exiled to the wilder parts of Ireland. A number of Borderers were pressed into military service and were posted to garrisons in the Low Countries and Ireland. Some, however, left of their own accord and found work in the towns, whilst others sold their skills as mercenaries on the Continent. Though the penalty for attempting to return from exile was death the Borderer was a hard man to keep down and many eventually slipped back to their old hunting grounds.

The habits of theft and violence died hard, and, in spite of the grim punishments for those apprehended, small groups of thieves known as Moss troopers still haunted the remoter Border regions until well into the 17th century. Riding with the moonlight, they "lifted" what they could, and in the tradition of their forefathers led the authorities a merry dance. But the old days, when 1,000 lances would thunder across the dark Border hills, were gone forever, and soon the mists of time closed around them all. It was indeed their "Last Goodnight".

opposite >

The Last Goodnight

The old days were gone forever, and, by the end of the 17th century, both the reiver and the Mosstrooper had passed into history and folklore.

This is my departing night,
For here nae langer must I stay;
There's neither friend or foe o' mine,
But wishes me away.

What I have done through lack of wit,
I never can recall;
I hope ye're a' my friends as yet;
Good night and joy be with you all!

Further reading:

Factual:

Calendar of Border Papers, Ed. J Bain
Border Raids and Reivers, R Borland
The Story of Redesdale, B Charlton
The Steel Bonnets, G M Fraser
Borderland Castles and Peles, R Hugill
Flodden; the Anglo Scottish War of 1513, C Kightly
The Illustrated Border Ballads, J Marsden
Border History, G Ridpath
Shielings and Bastles, H G Ramm, R W McDowell & E Mercer
The Rise and Fall of the English Highland Clans, R Robson
Last Years of a Frontier, D L Tough
The Border Reivers, G Watson

Fiction:

A Famine of Horses, P F Chisholm
A Season of Knives, P F Chisholm
A Surfeit of Guns, P F Chisholm
The Candlemas Road, G M Fraser
Martin Farrell, J Howker
The Hanging Tree, A Massie
Balefire, N Tranter

Museums:

The Border History Museum, The Old Gaol, Hexham, Northumberland

Drumlanrig's Tower, Hawick, Roxburgh, Scotland

Kelvingrove Museum, Glasgow, Scotland

Tullie House Museum, Carlisle, Cumbria

Visitors to the Border area may also want to obtain *In Search of the Border Reivers*, a map which shows all relevant sites of interest.